many types of wildflowers

many types of wildflowers ©2020 by **janelle cordero**. Published in the United States by Vegetarian Alcoholic Press. Not one part of this work may be reproduced without expressed written consent by the author. For more information, please contact vegalpress@gmail.com

Contents

I.

you're looking at a picture of you	7
pushing me down	8
a child fails the math test	9
petri dish	10
thick books	11
i'll have what i have now	12
my friend her mercy	13
boundaries	14
god's name	15
be quiet a while	16
remind me	17
what they say	18
god or not god	19

II.

many types of wildflowers	23
answers where there are none	24
empty	25
of equal feeling and sadness	26
a shallowing	27
stupid question	28
distant failure	29
the sky and the earth	30
everything is prayer	31
the same question	32
once the fear is settled	33
when i squint and look at you	34
separate lakes	35
a blossoming	36
all of its history	37
could be alive	38
made sense of all this	39
every moment	40

III.

the phone book	43
god reads the newspapers	44
dirt path	45
on the edge some blue	46
the rest of it	47
tuesday afternoon	48
every time the phone rings	49
some days	50
clothesline	51
i'm right here	52
step on someone else's tragedy	53
teeth	54
one word spoken in two different languages	55
between fear and longing	56
the dead	57

IV.

my sadness and my happiness	61
white dress red shoes	62
walking from one town to the next	63
disaster	64
the opposite of god	65
folded note	66
sleep talking	67
my reflections	68
nothing exists outside of god	69
which way from here	70
thoughts drain from our heads	71
birds outside	72
too much	73
simple as death	74
obsolete over time	75

I.

you're looking at a picture of you

say you're looking at a picture of you with a group of other people who / do you look at first yourself or / the other people say / you're a parent and you have a picture of your child who / do you look at first your child or the you within / your child maybe / god looks at us in the same way trying to see / only herself /

pushing me down

we are not born knowing tragedy so when / are we old enough to understand the
human capacity for causing and / experiencing suffering take / the home
video of me learning to walk and my three-year-old brother pushing
me down and he is the one / who cries as i hit / the ground /

a child fails the math test

there's talk of transplanting our memories into robots before we die as a way to live on how / little we understand of being human and / we're already trying to move beyond human the way / a child fails the math test on chapter 5 but / must still move on to chapter 6 /

petri dish

it's easy to believe in god if you don't try to believe / in all the other stuff like eternal life and angels it's easy / just to believe in a creating presence something like / a scientist who began the world as an experiment and then / left the petri dish to have dinner with the other gods we've been left alone / for a few hours maybe in god's time god is not negligent but / we are misunderstood and flailing all the same easy to believe / we'll destroy ourselves before god returns /

thick books

some mornings we wake with light thoughts but most of the time / we wake with heavy thoughts and we / balance them like thick books on top of our heads /

i'll have what i have now

i spend an unreasonable amount of time thinking about death because / science tells
me i will die and my body will decay i can be buried / in a mushroom suit that feeds
my decomposition to the fungi spores or i can be / buried in a pod that will grow
into a tree aboveground or / i can be burned and then spread in a body of water
like herbs shaken into a broth / the body does not survive and / religion tells
me the body will die dust to dust but / something beyond the body some /
essence of me is eternal and will / live on i want something in between
rot and forever something like / the 905 years given to enosh i know
everyone says this but i wouldn't / waste it maybe some days would
be spent just sunning in the grass but / the rest of the time i'll wake
up early to spend / hours at my desk reading manifestos and
studying the many / languages and religions of the world
i'll travel to every country and / i'll know and love so
many generations i'll have / what i have now but /
more so /

my friend her mercy

we were teenagers driving into town after a day / at the lake my friend my / best
friend at the time she / was driving we hit a bird some three miles out hard to /
remember but i think it was / a duck my friend stopped the car right away and
then backed the car up we / have to make sure it's dead she said i / protested
why make things worse the bird was / just a pile of brown feathers / un-
moving she drove over the bird with / one of the tires and we could /
feel its body under us the weight / of it crushed oh / how i
screamed how i failed to understand / my friend her /
mercy her / unblinking eye /

boundaries

we put so many boundaries between ourselves and the world like underwear
followed / by pants shirt and a heavy overcoat if / the air is cold we do not
want to feel it we think weather / has nothing to do with us so / we stay
out of it and we say things like / that's none of my business when it
comes to other people we only / get involved until things become
inconvenient then we say / this is your cross to bear we do not
understand / our shape in the world has no true boundary /
we overlap with all things and all people a sociologist said /
mature faith is recognizing god does not put our personal
needs or desires above / the needs or desires of others /

god's name

when one thing ends and another thing appears we find god / the jews have seventy-two mystical names for god all of which / are incorrect the moment we learn a new name for god it is no longer / god's name the same as when a secret is given away to the wrong person in this way / we are all the wrong people /

be quiet a while

be quiet a while to see / what you'll learn from a world / that is so loud and doesn't believe anyone / is paying attention /

remind me

remind me what spring feels like remind me / of how the ground thaws and the
hiking trails turn / muddy with snowmelt remind me of the / buttercups and
the glacier lilies that grow / in sunny spots on the hills and remind me / of
how the tree branches bud and leaves / unfurl remind me of how
the sun sets later and later in / the evenings and how the
mornings are still / brilliant with frost remind me of
how nothing lasts not / the flowers or the cold
mornings not / our bodies or our memories /
remind me that it is better not to
live forever /

what they say

bukowski didn't believe in god or at least he didn't readily / accept religion he felt there were too many strings attached but / he did believe in heaven because he knew his wife would wind up there some day and isn't / that true for most of us we can imagine / an afterlife for the people we love but for ourselves / it doesn't quite add up kind of like how / clothing on a mannequin looks just right but when we put the same outfit on the sleeves / are too short and the pants are too tight and the color / is all wrong maybe we're being too hard on ourselves but it's true what they say heaven / is for everybody else /

god or not god

every question i ask leads back to god or / not god / god is at the very center of us and god / is at the farthest reaches of the universe these locations are the same / god is an airplane overhead for / a moment and then moving on to / somewhere else / space is perfect / earth is not maybe / this alone is proof enough of god but / maybe not /

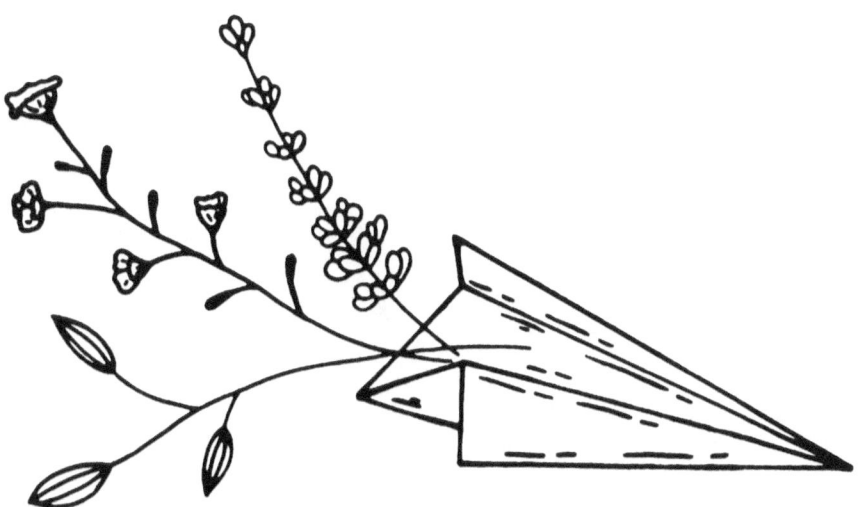

II.

many types of wildflowers

i believe in my religion the same way i believe / in all religions like a child trying / to make sense of the many types of wildflowers in a field and deciding / they are all the same because / they are all alive /

answers where there are none

the pastor tells me she has no expectations / of heaven no / inside knowledge no
hidden scriptures to / reveal what remains after death she hopes / to reunite
with loved ones but she doesn't know / what form that will take she's here
now / on earth and / that's what matters she / wants to make life better
for / the people around her / i thank her for not offering / answers
where there are none we'll let mystery be / mystery she says /
there's no need to ask / for more than we've already
been given /

empty

you are an empty space and the world / tries to fill you with car advertisements and political campaigns and the newest brand / of tennis shoes but what's wrong with / being empty think of how the wind would / move through you isn't that alone worth giving all the rest up /

of equal feeling and sadness

he forgot his wife's birthday once he tells us but / that was near the end he says / when nothing really mattered she's his / ex-wife now but / he still calls her at midnight on the morning / of her birthday to prove he'll never forget again / love is like any other form / of matter it never / disappears but rather changes into / something else of equal / feeling and sadness /

a shallowing

maybe death isn't deep and wet and cloying like / a well maybe death is /
a shallowing a / drying up / think of the pond that forms / in the valley
from snowmelt in the spring think of how / it shrinks with each hot /
summer day by august / it's gone maybe our lives / are like that /

stupid question

a young woman sits on the steps in the alley behind / the piano store where i take
lessons she asks me / for a cigarette and i say / sorry i don't smoke she /
says thanks anyway and puts her head between / her knees the way
we're supposed to during plane crashes i ask her / if she's alright
but she doesn't respond probably because /
it was a stupid question /

distant failure

the jewish poet says we are all / swallowed by the earth good and evil together / he has no hope for the afterlife and his poems / describe god as a distant failure / someone who has forgotten us here the way / some house plants are forgotten in a dark corner how / quickly they wither /

the sky and the earth

the sky and the earth are not divided but / we keep them that way in our minds so we do not / go insane /

everything is a prayer

prayer lives in us even when we give it / no voice or attention see the way we lift
our hands to the sky on / a warm summer day see the way we watch children in
the street and smile when they / walk by with their ice creams dripping down
the fronts of their shirts their laughter and teasing of one another proves /
something about our own childhoods life was really / as good as we
remember back then and we wish / the summer stays pleasant and
unmarred for their sake see / everything is a prayer when our
minds and hearts agree /

the same question

sometimes i wish i lived centuries ago when / more people believed in god and / it would've been easier for me to believe but / this is cowardly and lazy all i have / to do is spend the rest of my life asking / the same question to come / to an answer that never stays / the same /

once the fear is settled

the fear of death comes on less and less and / when it does i know what / to do
i say honey / you're here now and / that's enough i / speak to myself this way /
determined to be kind the kindness / soothes the panic and i find myself
nodding i am / here now i am here / now the rest of it / the great
mystery i've been afraid of / all my life will be revealed soon
enough / once the fear is settled i go on /

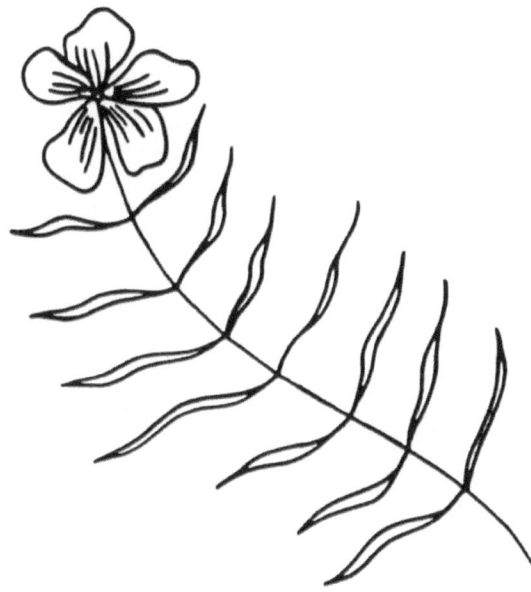

when i squint and look at you

when i say the word you i mean / the universe inside of you when i / squint and look at you in the sun your body / is made of light and then i open my eyes wide and your body / is something solid again do you understand / you're both /

separate lakes

the internal world and the external world are / separate lakes fed by the same stream /

a blossoming

he said what if / instead of gravestones we plant trees above the bodies i said / i'd
like to be a lilac tree he said / avocado the woman next to him said / hemlock
we're already willing to give up being human / for something else the
woman we all know has cancer said / nothing she's too close /
to death to see it as a blossoming /

all of its history

strange to think bodies were once / walked from the funeral home to the gravesite the weight / of the casket seems untruthful shouldn't the body / weigh next to nothing without the soul and all / of its history /

could be alive

he was found along the railroad tracks downtown in / may of 1971 white /
man in his sixties wearing a long / brown coat and green pants here's
something a tattoo / on his right forearm that could be / a name but
it's unreadable / there's even a picture of / the body naked from /
the waist up his eyes are closed thank / god the skin on his neck
is puckered around / a raised white scar / receding hairline
wide mouth with / lips the same color as his skin he looks
like someone i could know he looks like / someone who
could be / alive is what i'm saying /

made sense of all this

ray carver was only fifty when he died of / lung cancer do we have more to say
when we get older what other lessons / did carver have to teach us i read /
his poems and think of him as / a friend though i was born years / after
his death tell me / carver / how do you spend your days now what do /
you think of when thinking is all that's left i wish / you could've grown
older i wish / you could've made sense of all this for me /

every moment

what makes most sense to you / never or always / eternity exists in both / eternity exists / in every moment we give / our full attention to /

III.

the phone book

the phone book used to be validation for our existence are you / listed we would ask each other and the unlisted / were like ghosts we couldn't understand why anyone / wouldn't want their name and their number alongside all / those other names and numbers can we have meaning / beyond our connection to others here's the real / question if we leave no evidence of ourselves is the world / better for it /

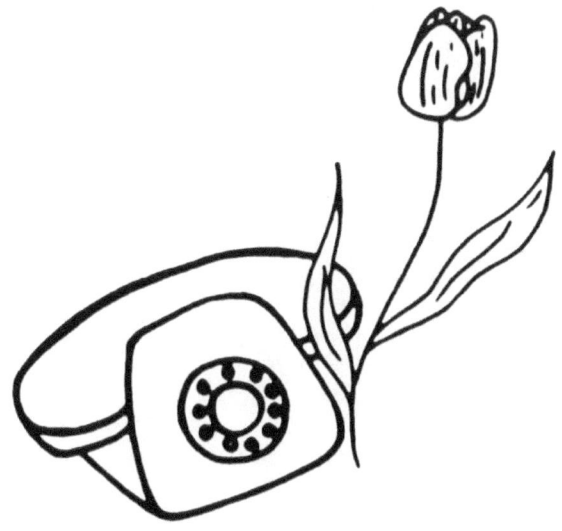

god reads the newspapers

maybe god reads the newspapers to keep up on / just how bad things are getting the dailies are like / humanity's report card and if we start failing everything she will / intervene with a famine or a prophet something / to knock us off our feet something / to remind us we are not in control /

dirt path

the men in the asylum spend their days / walking a pre-determined circle around / the building stopping only / to use the bathroom their feet have worn / a dirt path into the sod the circle / does not cure them but at least / they feel like they are / moving forward /

on the edges some blue

i wake up in the dark and look / at the clock just past five i walk / to the back porch to find the first frost / of the season glinting on the lawn the sky is mostly / black but on the edges some blue some / promise for the day ahead i go back inside to make coffee and / wait for the morning paper to be delivered one / by one the lights of neighbor's houses click on as / we all join the world /

the rest of it

early morning almost autumn the neighborhood dogs begin their off-tune and tragic
howling the teenagers / are playing baseball at the school a block away as the
garbage trucks / move up and down our alleyways collecting a lifetime's
worth of waste in their mechanical mouths the mailman / puts more
garbage into our mailboxes and life goes on / like this until snowfall
when baseball stops but not / the rest of it /

tuesday afternoon

most of the people in the world could care less how i spend / this tuesday afternoon
so why does it matter so much whether i leave the house or stay sitting / on the
porch for another few hours here's the secret we are much / less important
than we imagine so i'll spend my day the way i like / alone and without
any checklists or people getting mixed up with / the quiet /

every time the phone rings

i get the feeling not everybody is as anxious around phones as i am here's the thing /
it's not the phone itself that worries me but the possibility of / a call i don't want
to be on the receiving end of / usually somebody asking for something / like my
time or my money or sometimes my advice / on a personal matter each of us /
only has so many resources so much energy and once / those things are
depleted there's no building them back / up again i'm telling you the
truth so don't go running every time / the phone rings make the
bastards wait a while before / they suck you dry /

some days

some days i leave the phone off and keep / the curtains closed some days i don't
answer the door even if / someone has been out there knocking for / five
minutes or more some days i don't / check the mailbox or even go
outside some days are meant / to be spent alone with the
houseplants and / my own mind with / its many
passageways some days have / no room for the
crowd out there and on / days like that hardly
anyone tries to contact me it's like / they can
sense it they can / sense how lonely i need
to be /

clothesline

we think / of time as a line stretched tight from one end of existence to / the other but consider a clothesline the thin rope wrapped / around two posts and weighed down by flannel shirts and jeans given body by / the wind the center of the rope is bowed towards the ground frayed and / ready to snap /

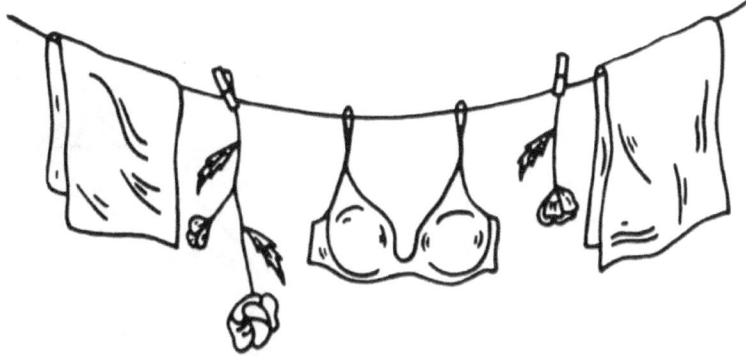

i'm right here

the physical feels more real than the unphysical or the metaphysical the footsteps /
in the apartment above my head are the sound of god / ignoring me sometimes / i
tap the handle of a broomstick on the ceiling to try and get her attention but / she
just keeps walking from one room to another probably looking / for something
the same way we search for our keys or the letter from our great aunt we
meant to answer but / didn't god wouldn't have keys or a great aunt
so / what could she be looking for i'm right here i want to
shout / i'm right here /

step on someone else's tragedy

i'm standing on a sidewalk far from my home but still / in the same city a woman
walks up to me and says / my brother was murdered right where / you're
standing my eyes go wide and i look down for spots of blood on the
concrete / four years ago she says and i look / back at her
she's not / crying not even close i say i'm sorry she says / you
didn't kill him i ask who did she says / someone who thought
her brother was someone else my god / i say and shake my
head how can you / make sense of that she says / she can't
she shrugs and puts / a flower down on the concrete right
in front of me some kind of / tulip that could grow in
anyone's back yard and then / she walks away i
worry about the flower and how / it could get
trampled or stolen or blown away in the wind
but / maybe that's the point every day / we
step on someone else's tragedy the woman
does not / look back and soon / i walk
away too /

teeth

we hardly saw our neighbor after all / his teeth fell out he was embarrassed about it but / we didn't care he finally started smoking / on his porch again come summertime and we were careful not to mention / anything related to teeth instead we / gave him shit about his overgrown lawn and he teased us for using an old-fashioned push mower the thing / doesn't even have a motor just spinning blades we'd say / goodbye and when we got / the car doors shut we talked about his teeth as we drove away waving to him / the whole time /

one word spoken in two different languages

we cannot be separated into the living and the dying because / we are all dying there's a closeness / between life and death like one word spoken / in two different languages my husband / wakes up at 2 am sometimes and his first thought is / i'm going to die and his second / thought is what have i done with my life and / his third thought is / not much and all the while i'm sleeping beside him my body breathing / all on its own /

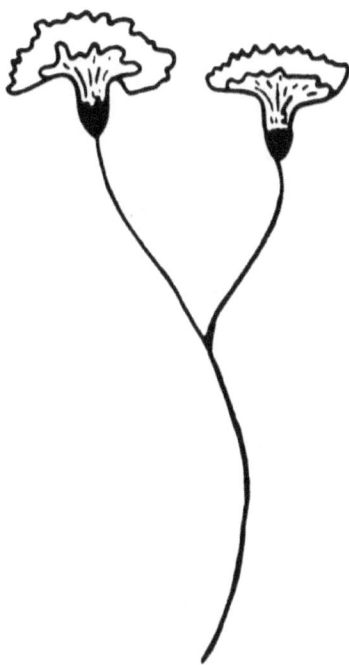

between fear and longing

there's a difference between fear and longing i used to be / afraid of death because of what it would mean / for me my memories my soul that sort / of thing now i simply long for / more time with this world i've grown / to love remember / what the great spiritual teachers have said heaven / is inside of us /

the dead

the dead do not carry ripped pages of scripture in their jean pockets they do not / make coffee in the morning they do not / feel tired or awake they do not / drive cars they have nowhere to go and nothing to do the dead / do not believe in anything not even the living the same way / we do not believe in them /

IV.

my sadness and my happiness

my sadness is so similar to my happiness like / the same dress in a different color /

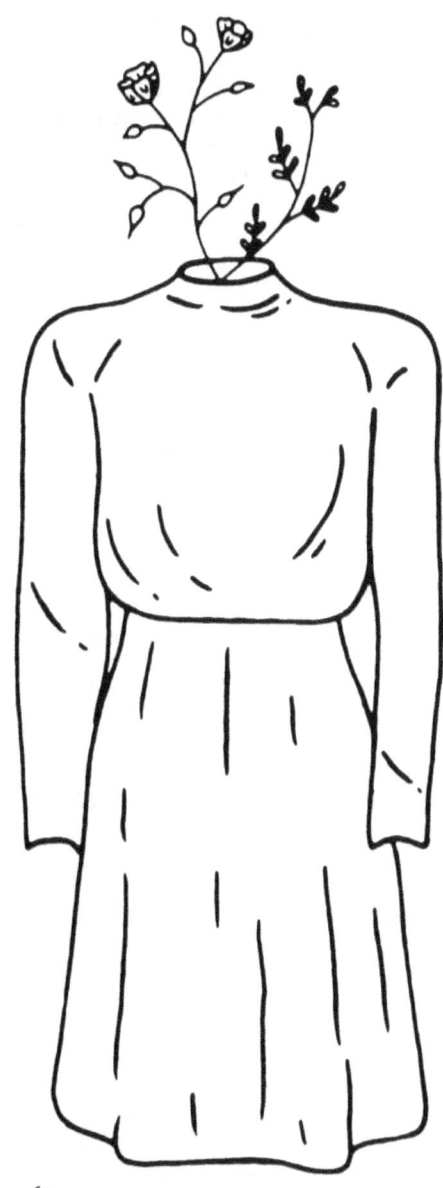

white dress red shoes

there's a picture of me as a little girl in a white dress and red shoes on my first day
of preschool and / there's a picture of me as a woman in a white dress and red
shoes on my wedding day both pictures / sit side-by-side on my mother's
mantle as proof / of my many selves or as proof of the one self with /
many bodies i wonder if my mother misses one of me more / than
the others i was not / an affectionate child but when i cried / i
needed comfort same / as everyone maybe she liked
comforting me or maybe she prefers me / as an
adult more like a friend someone / to have
conversations with does being a parent /
mean always grieving for what time has
taken or / does it mean looking forward
to meeting who your child / will
become /

walking from one town to the next

the days of my life are like walking from one town to the next except / the towns have the same name and the path / i follow is a circle this is not / because my days are the same but because / i am the same /

disaster

barely 40 degrees but / the sun is out and the skies are blue so / i sit on my back
porch in jeans and / a long sleeve shirt i / wrap my arms around myself when
the wind comes on i / listen to the birds sing of what lies ahead / disaster
for all i know but / these birds make everything sound so sweet /

the opposite of god

we know more than the dead but does that make us / any better off the opposite of god is not / the devil who i don't believe in the opposite of god / is the absence of god which is easiest for me to believe in the opposite of me / is still me /

folded note

god is mostly subtle sending me / quiet messages like a child slipping / a folded note to another child behind / the teacher's back /

sleep talking

i talk in my sleep and will often / sit up in bed frightened over something that may / or may not exist you are / patient with me you say / everything will be okay you get out of our bed to check / the house for spirits real or imagined and when / you return i'm asleep again flat / on my back and silent where does / speech come from when we / are not in control /

my reflections

alone in the house aside from my reflections / in the windows and they make / poor company because i get the feeling / i'm not real to them /

nothing exists outside of god

we can choose to be one thing or / we can choose to be all things / it's a matter of perspective why / do we look up to see god we could / just as easily look side to side or down / at our feet we could close our eyes to see god too and / never open them again do you / understand nothing exists outside of / god
nothing exists / nothing /

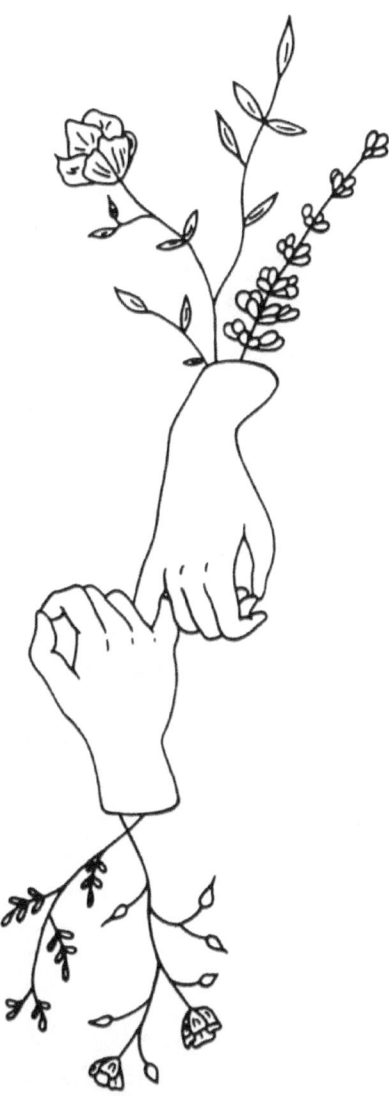

which way from here

we always ask / which way from here as if / we were never meant to stay in a place longer / than we want to / we tell our shadows to guide us when / shadows know even less of the world and / its intentions /

thoughts drain from our heads

the world is made for equal parts / resting and doing but / here we are thinking only of the doing and giving / little thought to laying down in the middle / of the day and letting our thoughts drain from / our heads gently like water / from our ears after a good swim /

birds outside

not silence but stillness not / stillness but the quiet rise and fall of / your chest in
another room here are / the sounds your breath / somewhere my breath
somewhere and the refrigerator with / its slow mechanical hum what
does it mean to be / alone but not alone i close my eyes and / hear
birds outside have they / been here all along /

too much

what is eternity if not / everything we've already experienced who can / name every memory since birth see / we've already been given / too much /

simple as death

the woods are quiet i hear / only my footsteps and my / breathing if i inhale through my mouth i can / taste the cold and the cedar trees tiny flakes of / snow are falling but / it's hard to say if they come from the sky or / the tree branches prayer doesn't come easy / anymore so instead i / turn my mind into the still surface of a lake with / no wind i become the great / emptiness we are all so afraid of the routine is / as simple as death /

obsolete over time

the body is a machine that is perfect in the beginning and becomes / obsolete over time like / any good piece of technology or like any / good god of childhood /

Acknowledgments

"i'll have what i have now" first published in Aurora Journal

"you're looking at a picture of you," "the phone book," and "many types of wildflowers" first published in Silver Pinion

"a shallowing" first published in Vagabond City

"disaster," "birds outside," and "once the fear is settled" first published in Where Is the River

"my friend her mercy," "of equal feeling and sadness," and "simple as death" first published in Papeachu Review

"remind me" first published in Yes Poetry

"my sadness and my happiness," "obsolete over time," and "the sky and the earth" first published in A Glimpse Of

www.ingramcontent.com/pod-product-compliance
Lightning Source LLC
Chambersburg PA
CBHW030350100526
44592CB00010B/902